The Multiplying Menace
DIVIDES

A Math Adventure

Pam Calvert

Illustrated by Wayne Geehan

Charlesbridge

For my brother, Norman, and sister, Kathy.
I love you both the same—
it can't be divided!—P. C.

For my daughter Amy, the Geehan
Family Mathemagician—W. G.

Text copyright © 2011 by Pam Calvert
Illustrations copyright © 2011 by Wayne Geehan

Published by Charlesbridge
85 Main Street
Watertown, MA 02472
(617) 926-0329
www.charlesbridge.com

Library of Congress Cataloging-in-Publication Data
Calvert, Pam, 1966–
    The multiplying menace divides / Pamela Calvert ; Illustrations by Wayne Geehan.
      p. cm.
    Summary: Prince Peter uses division to outwit a witch named Matilda and
Rumpelstiltskin who are threatening to destroy the entire kingdom. Includes math
notes about dividing by whole numbers and by fractions.
    ISBN 978-1-57091-781-3 (reinforced hardcover)
    ISBN 978-1-57091-782-0 (softcover)
[1. Division—Fiction. 2. Multiplication—Fiction. 3. Characters in literature—Fiction.
4. Magic—Fiction.] I. Geehan, Wayne, ill. II. Title.
PZ7.C138Mv 2011   [Fic]—dc22 2010007583

Printed in China
(hc) 10 9 8 7 6 5 4 3 2 1
(sc) 10 9 8 7 6 5 4 3 2 1

Illustrations done in acrylic paint on canvas
Display type and text type set in ITC Kallos and Dante MT
Color separations by Chroma Graphics, Singapore
Printed and bound September 2010 by Yangjiang Millenium Litho Ltd.
  in Yangjiang Guangdong, China
Production supervision by Brian G. Walker
Designed by Martha MacLeod Sikkema

"Zero!" Prince Peter yelled, but there was no sign of his dog or the multiplying stick that Zero had dug up earlier in the morning. He tried not to think about what would happen if the enchanted stick fell into evil hands again.

As Peter passed a farm, he noticed ten cows and five froggy cows grazing in the field. One froggy cow stopped chewing its cud and mooed a ribbity moo.

"What is the farmer feeding them?" Peter wondered.

3

When he neared town a lady ran past him, screaming, "Two of my children are frogs!" Peter stared as two child-sized frogs hopped around the woman and six children.

"Nah, it couldn't be . . . he's been banished," he said to himself.
Still he headed back to the castle to tell his father, the king, about
the strange frog sightings.

Peter greeted the twelve knights who guarded the castle gate. Suddenly the ground shook and . . .

FLASH!

Four frogs in shining armor appeared where knights had once stood.

"Has Rumpelstiltskin returned?" Peter asked himself. He would never forget how Rumpelstiltskin had wreaked havoc on the kingdom with the multiplying stick.

Heart pounding, he bolted to the throne room.

The queen sat crying with a large frog on her lap.

"Where's Father?" Peter asked.

"He's a frog . . . again."

"Again?" Peter said.

"Yes, when he was a prince, a witch named Matilda turned him into a frog. A princess broke the spell with a kiss. I tried, but kissing won't work this time."

"Wait . . . a princess kissed Father?"

"Once upon a time, before he met me—but that's another story."

"Oh. . . . So, this isn't Rumpelstiltskin's mischief?"

"No. Your father's twelve advisors are searching for Matilda now," the Queen said, walking onto the balcony.

"Father has twenty-four advisors. What happened to the other twelve?"

"They're frogs, too," she sobbed.

Peter gulped. With the magic multiplying stick, if twenty-four advisors were multiplied by one-half, then twelve would be left and the other twelve would disappear. Except this time frogs were part of the equation. How could people be reduced to frogs? Was this some sort of diabolical amphibian division? Something had to be done!

Peter headed for the Royal Swamp, but all he found there were ordinary frogs. Just as he was about to give up, Peter heard a familiar cackle from a nearby cave. He tiptoed toward it and listened.

"Matilda, your Frog Crystal is creating more chaos than the Great Divide could do on its own," Rumpelstiltskin said.

"Soon we'll divide the whole kingdom into frogs!" the witch screeched.

Divide, but how? Peter wondered. His eyes widened as he spied Rumpelstiltskin gazing into a glowing, green stone. There was a stick in Rumpelstiltskin's hand, but the symbol at the end wasn't an x—it was a line between two dots.

"Yes, then we'll each have our revenge on the king and his meddlesome son for getting us trapped in the Abyss of Zero," Rumpelstiltskin cackled.

"Who would have thought that your old algebra lessons would help rescue us from that awful place?" Matilda said.

"Wait until I get my hands on that prince. I'll teach *him* a lesson. . . ."

"Rumpel, you promised him to me! Frog princes are all the rage, according to *In Stye* magazine." She thrust the pages under his nose. "Eating them is good for your skin. Not to mention delicious. . . ."

INSTYE
Home and Hovel Magazine

POSH PRINCE
MAKES TASTY DISH

5 Reasons Why
Your BEAUTY
Depends on it!

HOG and FROG
Recipes . . . page 48

Love Potion in 5 min.

"Never fear, Matilda, you'll have your prince . . . NOW!"
In a flash Rumpelstiltskin appeared behind Peter and pushed him toward Matilda.

"Let me go!" Peter cried.

"Ooh, he's a feisty one—just like his father is," Matilda crowed, licking her lips. "I have a special recipe in mind for him."

Rumpelstiltskin laughed. "First I need something from the boy."

"He's mine!" Matilda howled. "I have a craving for Frog Prince stew."

"Matilda, he has the Great Multiplier. When it's combined with the Great Divide, you can have anything you want—we'll have unlimited math power!" Then Rumpelstiltskin grumbled, "And I'll let you use it first."

"Divine," Matilda cackled, turning to Peter. "Tell us where the Great Multiplier is!"

"Never!" Peter yelled.

"Maybe this will change your mind." Rumpelstiltskin waved the Great Divide over the Frog Crystal. It cast an image of Zero sniffing trash in an alley near the castle. "Dog divided by one!" Instantly Zero morphed into a frog dog.

"Change him back!" Peter cried.

"Give me the Great Multiplier, and I will," Rumpelstiltskin said.

"Can't you find it with your crystal?" Peter asked.

"The crystal can only see living things, dearie," Matilda said. "I'm a witch, not a miracle worker!"

"Like ribbiting cows happen every day?" Peter muttered to himself. Thinking quickly, he said aloud, "I need your help to find the alley where my dog is. Only Zero knows where the multiplier is buried." He hoped his ruse worked; he knew where the alley was but needed a chance to get the Great Divide away from Rumpelstiltskin.

"Very well," said Rumpelstiltskin, securing the Frog Crystal to the end of the dividing stick. "But one false move and I'll make you croak. Forever."

Matilda cackled. "Rumpel, you're a hoot."

As Peter followed the devious duo, Rumpelstiltskin continued his reign of chaos. "Butcher and wife divided by two!" he yelled. Suddenly the wife turned into a large frog wife and croaked loudly at her stunned husband.

How does he know what number to divide by? Peter wondered. Then they came upon a little girl playing with twelve kittens.

"Kittens divided by three," Rumpelstiltskin said. Four of the twelve became froggy kittens.

Watching the mewling kittens and their croaking siblings squirm together into smaller groups, Peter thought, *Yes! Twelve kittens can be divided into three sets of four. Rumpelstiltskin is dividing people and animals into groups . . . and one group is turning into frogs!*

As they neared town, Rumpelstiltskin pointed the Great Divide at a stable boy who was leading a horse to its stall.

"Rumpel, I want a turn," Matilda whined.

"You don't know how to use it," Rumpelstiltskin said.

Matilda grabbed the stick. "How hard can it be? See that horse? Watch!" She pointed the Great Divide at it. "Horse divided by one-fourth!" Instantly four small froggy horses leaped after the frightened stable boy.

Peter scratched his head. *Why did dividing by a fraction produce more froggy horses rather than fewer?* Then he noticed the froggy horses were about one-fourth, or one-quarter, the size of the original horse. It was as if the one horse had been divided into four quarter horses.

"Give the wand back!" Rumpelstiltskin lunged at Matilda.

She jumped out of the way, chiming, "This is fun!" Pointing the stick at two piglets, she incanted, "Piglets divided by one-fifth!" Ten tiny froggy piglets ribbity-oinked. Matilda stared at them and drooled. "All these frogs are making me hungry. . . ."

Taking advantage of the moment, Rumpelstiltskin yanked the Frog Crystal from the stick. "Enough with the frogs!" he yelled.

Matilda screamed, threw aside the Great Divide, and tackled Rumpelstiltskin. As they fought, Peter grabbed the stick and escaped.

Peter ran to the alley where he'd seen Zero in the crystal. Zero whimpered a ribbity woof. "Can you show me where you buried the multiplying stick?" Peter asked. Zero ribbited three times and hopped away.

Zero led Peter to one of his favorite burying spots. There
were fifteen covered holes. "Zero, with the Great Divide I can
reduce the number of holes and find the Great Multiplier before
Rumpelstiltskin and Matilda find us," Peter said.

Peter counted five rows of holes in groups of three. "I could
divide fifteen by five to get three holes . . . or, wait. . . ." Peter
aimed the Great Divide and said, "Holes divided by fifteen."
One hole remained.

All at once Rumpelstiltskin and Matilda appeared. They wrestled the Great Divide from Peter.

"Thought you could get away?" Rumpelstiltskin sneered. "Where is the Great Multiplier?"

"It's in that hole," Peter said.

Quickly Rumpelstiltskin dug out the multiplier.

"Now change Zero back as you promised," Peter insisted.

"Not yet." With the symbols at opposite ends, Rumpelstiltskin connected the Great Multiplier to the Great Divide. Fire crackled along the stick, causing Rumpelstiltskin to drop it. When the smoke cleared, a shimmering golden staff remained.

"Now I have complete operation power!" Rumpelstiltskin yelled as he reattached the Frog Crystal to the staff.

Matilda grabbed the staff from Rumpelstiltskin's hand.

"Are you mad?" Rumpelstiltskin bellowed. "You don't know how to use the Great Staff of Product-Quo." Fear crept into Rumpelstiltskin's voice. "One bad equation could destroy the staff, along with all our magic!"

"You promised I could use it first!" Matilda shrieked.

"Yes, but I didn't mean it," Rumpelstiltskin mumbled.

"Rumpel, it's time for us to divide the entire kingdom into frogs as we planned," Matilda said, cackling.

Peter's heart lurched. How could he stop Rumpelstiltskin and
Matilda? Then suddenly Zero began hopping around Matilda,
flicking his tongue at the stick.

"Get Zero away from me," Matilda yelled swinging the staff at
the dog. "I will not be deterred from my division quest!"

"Zero!" Peter called, and then a thought occurred to him.
Would dividing someone by zero send them back to the Abyss of Zero?
After all, multiplying by zero had worked to banish Rumpelstiltskin.

Peter thought some more. *Division divides things into groups or pieces. But how could a whole number be divided into groups of zero? The equation would make no sense. Was that what Rumpelstiltskin meant by "a bad equation"? Maybe it would destroy the staff.* Peter decided it was worth a try.

"Matilda," Peter said, "Quick! Divide Rumpelstiltskin by zero. Then you'd have the staff all to yourself."

"It's a trick!" Rumpelstiltskin cried, trying to get past Zero to reach Matilda.

A wicked smile swept over the witch's face. "Good try but I need Rumpel around. Besides I have a better idea." She pointed the staff at Peter's dog. "Zero divided by . . ."

"NO!" Peter yelled, reaching out to Zero.

"You can't . . ." Rumpelstiltskin screamed, as he grabbed for the staff.

But he was too late. "ZERO!" Matilda cried. The staff exploded, bursting the Frog Crystal into a shower of green sparks. Zero instantly turned back into a dog. The magic was vanquished. But when the green sparks hit Rumpelstiltskin and Matilda, the two fiends turned into frogs and hopped away.

"We did it, Zero!" Peter cheered.

Everyone celebrated the defeat of Rumpelstiltskin and Matilda. Peter's parents honored him as a great mathemagician and encouraged him to learn more feats of arithmagic. They also awarded Zero a burying area all his own.

As for Rumpelstiltskin and Matilda, they were swamped with problems that would keep them infinitely busy.

DIVISION NOTES

Division is an operation that divides something into equal groups or parts of a whole. The number that's divided is called the *dividend*. The number of equal groups is called the *divisor*. And the amount in each group is called the *quotient*.

$$6 \quad \div \quad 2 \quad = \quad 3$$

dividend   divisor   quotient

Dividing by Fractions

Since you're dividing into equal groups or parts, why does dividing by a fraction make a larger number? Because you are asking how many parts can fit into an amount. For example, when you divide three blocks by one-fifth, you are seeing how many "one-fifth" pieces can fit into three blocks. The answer is fifteen.

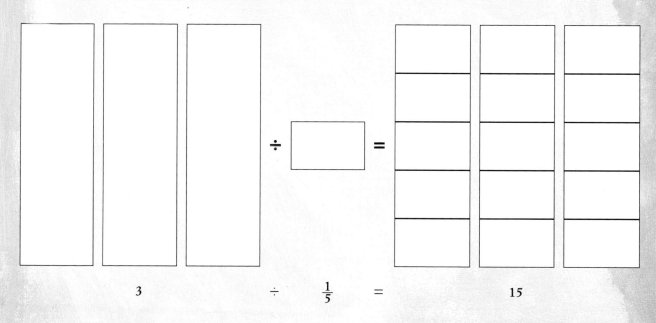

3          $\div$ $\frac{1}{5}$ $=$ 15

A fast way to calculate this is to multiply by the fraction's *reciprocal*, or opposite. To get a fraction's reciprocal, invert it (flip it upside down). For example, $\frac{5}{1}$ is the reciprocal of $\frac{1}{5}$. In the block problem, you could multiply like this:

$$3 \times \frac{5}{1} = 15$$

(reciprocal of $\frac{1}{5}$)

Dividing by Zero

Take five blocks and divide them by zero:

$$5 \div 0 = ?$$

How many groups of zero blocks will you need to equal five?

$$0 + 0 + 0 + 0 + 0 = 0$$

No matter how many groups of zero you add, you will never get five. As a result most mathematicians say that division by zero is *undefined*, meaning there is no sensible answer.